*What sort of people ought you to be
in lives of holiness and godliness, waiting for
and hastening the coming of the day of God…
for new heavens and a new earth
in which righteousness dwells.*

2 PETER 3:11-13

Celebrate Salvation!®

Heaven
Our Ultimate Destiny

F - Living faithful lives into eternity

The Joy of Christian Discipleship Series
Book 7

Dr. Bill Morehouse

His Kingdom Press

About Dr. Bill Morehouse

Dr. Morehouse was raised in a traditional Christian home in the 1950's and functionally became a humanist during college and medical school in the 1960's. After completing his medical residency in Family Medicine in the early 1970's he embarked on a career of serving the poor but soon found that his secular faith and alternative lifestyle were woefully inadequate to the task.

In 1974 he underwent a dramatic conversion from the philosophy and lifestyle he had been living to a wholehearted commitment to Jesus as his LORD and Savior. After returning to medicine and marrying in 1975, he and his wife dedicated themselves to growing in faith, raising their family of four children (plus spouses and grandchildren), and providing Christ-centered service to some of the most disadvantaged members of their community.

Since retiring from active clinical practice in July 2018, Dr. Morehouse has devoted himself to continued Christian growth, family, study, writing, and teaching about the Kingdom of God. He has had long personal and professional experience with the material covered in Celebrate Salvation.®

Heaven: Our Ultimate Destiny

Copyright 2023 by William R. Morehouse
ISBN: 978-1-7353899-7-4 (paperback)
Web Address: www.celebratesalvation.org

His Kingdom Press
Rochester, New York 14619

Special discounts are available on quantity purchases by corporations, associations, educators, and others. For details, contact the publisher through www.hiskingdom.us/press.

Heaven Contents

Background Material

Heaven: Our Ultimate Destiny

Acknowledgements

The work you have in your hands is part of a deeply rooted and ongoing collaboration that extends back for generations and even millennia. Jesus came to reveal God's love to struggling mankind and to demonstrate the depth of that love in ways that have had a profound impact on countless lives and entire societies ever since. He embodied the fullness of God in human form and called us out of darkness, confusion, and bondage into the wonderful light, clarity, and freedom we were created to inhabit.

We start out so fresh and pure as infants but soon become soiled and spoiled. Then as the years go by we get deeper and deeper into life's inevitable corruptions. As the Psalmist wrote:

> The LORD *looks down from heaven on the children of man, to see if there are any who understand, who seek after God. They have all turned aside; together they have become corrupt; there is none who does good, not even one.*
>
> Psalm 14:2-3, also noted in Psalm 53:1-3 and Romans 3:10-12

Can we reverse this process and become clean again? Do you believe in second, third, and even seven times seventieth chances? God does.

Historically, there were entire eras when certain troubling human conditions like discrimination, injustice, and poverty, were just written off as hopeless. This work owes a deep debt of gratitude to the God who can save and sanctify us, as well as to fellow believers in the Body of Christ and others who have been and are working tirelessly to reveal and share the truth that God hears our prayers and is patiently revealing His Kingdom in our midst, within our hearts and around us in our communities.

Many people are continuing to contribute their prayers, thoughts, ideas, and constructive comments to the growth and development of Celebrate Salvation.® I am particularly grateful to the pioneering work of generations of those who have gone before me as well as to many contributors in my local church fellowship and beyond. I would especially like to honor my wife and life partner, Susan, for her unfailing love and support over the decades we have been given to share life, faith, family, and community together.

Meeting 21st Century Needs, Part 2

We are increasingly living in an age of confusion about truth and falsehood. Who is telling the truth, and can we really tell the difference? Enlightenment misunderstandings about the governments of men and of God, Postmodernism, Eastern mysticism, blurred messaging in the faith community, questions about life after death and the reality of heaven and hell, and the blending of secular with spiritual definitions of terms like freedom, liberty, and justice… What does our faith have to offer? As the prophet noted,

Justice is turned back, and righteousness stands far away; for truth has stumbled in the public squares, and uprightness cannot enter.   Isaiah 59:14

In an attempt to address the need for guidance that an increasing number are searching for, Celebrate Salvation® has developed a broad-based Christ-centered study series and discipleship program designed to reach a wide audience of sincere seekers. Are you yearning for truth in our troubled age, a new believer seeking to be established in your faith, someone who has recently renewed your faith commitment in Christ and wants to revitalize your faith and ability to be an effective witness to others, or a church leader committed to equipping your congregation for growth? If so, our courses may help you find what you are seeking.

Celebrate Salvation's® underlying design began with a time-honored set of biblical steps to living faith very clearly outlined during a time of revival in the early 20th Century by the Oxford Group. One outgrowth of this movement became the well-known 12-Steps and Traditions of AA which have been instrumental in helping millions find God-given strength to overcome addictive behaviors. In the 1990s the 12-Step approach was significantly reframed by John Baker and Rick Warren at Saddleback Church into a clearly Christian program called Celebrate Recovery® (CR) which is compatible with its Oxford Group roots and applicable to a wider array of common human difficulties.

Over the years, many have observed that Step programs capture the essential and lifelong biblical dynamics involved in becoming a spiritually born-again believer and active disciple of Jesus Christ. Sadly, apart from programs like AA and CR, struggles with pornography and other negative or destructive attitudes or behaviors that impair many people's lives are often not covered in church gatherings, pulpit messages, or new member classes. Perhaps it's because people may be reluctant to be open about potentially embarrassing problems or congregations may lack the capacity to handle them. Access to faith-based Christian growth and discipleship resources for helping members and new believers overcome personal issues and become solidly established in their faith may also be limited.

Many of us also find ourselves aching for an outpouring of God's Holy Spirit, for times of widespread revival and spiritual awakening. Are we prepared? What would happen if God were to answer our prayers and pour out His Spirit throughout our communities, breaking open those already in the church and bringing in a large influx of new believers laden with the issues of our modern world? Would we and our churches know how to handle a Great Awakening like this? Celebrate Salvation® has taken the Oxford Group's steps, as modified by 12-Step and CR programs, and clarified them further with grateful credit to make them available to the church at large in a series of study guides organized into two courses and a devotional as listed on Page 61.

Course 1: Established in 3 Stages (A, B, C) and 7 Steps builds on the work of the Oxford Group and covers the foundational process of becoming established as a disciple of Jesus who is saved by His grace, committed to ongoing sanctification, and ready to live out His Great Commission with purity, integrity, and enthusiasm.

Course 2: Equipped in 3 Realms (D, E, F) and 7 Understandings goes beyond the foundational studies of Course 1 by helping group members understand how to cooperate with God as He brings spiritual awakening to individuals, churches, and entire communities; advances His Kingdom in our midst; and continually undergirds us with assurances about our future beyond the grave as well as between now and then.

Discovering the ever-unfolding mystery of faith in the living God is a wonderfully profound, life-changing, and satisfying gift. Our hope is that this modest series of introductory studies will provide a biblically balanced and comprehensive understanding of our faith which is widely applicable, reproducible, and fruitful. Please use the materials in *The Joy of Christian Discipleship Series* and augment them with those of your own fellowship group as we seek to meet the needs of our time with God's faithful Word.

Dr. Bill Morehouse
August 2023

Meeting 21st Century Needs, Part 2

Celebrate Salvation!®
The Joy of Christian Discipleship Course 2
Equipped in 3 Realms with 7 Understandings

Awakening: The Triumph of Truth
D - Waking up into the Light of God

1. **Natural birth and growth:** The processes of birth, becoming aware and oriented, growing, learning, and maturing through the natural stages of life.

2. **Spiritual birth and discipleship:** Similarities between natural growth processes and those of spiritual rebirth, awakening to spiritual realities, and growing in discipleship.

3. **Awakening of faith in communities:** The dynamics and social consequences of spiritual awakening in groups and broader segments of society.

Kingdom: God's Reign in our Midst
E - His Kingdom, here now and forever

4. **What is a kingdom?** Understanding where we fit in the authority and social structures around us, including models of family, church, community, education, industry, and government.

5. **Our dual citizenship:** How to live fruitful lives simultaneously in the temporal kingdoms of this world and the eternal Kingdom of God.

6. **The Millennial Kingdom and beyond:** Anticipating Christ's second coming, millennial reign, and final judgment while living in the realities of today's world.

Heaven: Our Ultimate Destiny
F - Living faithful lives into eternity

7. **Our eternal home:** Casting a vision of where we will be after we die and how we can live our lives between now and then. The **Destination**, **Transition**, and **Journey**.

Background Material

About Course 2

Similar to the material in Course 1 of *The Joy of Christian Discipleship Series*, **Course 2** has been developed as three books to complete our series: the first is about the ***Awakening*** of living faith, the second our citizenships in the world and the ***Kingdom*** of God, and the third our ultimate destiny as inheritors of eternal life extending into ***Heaven***. These workbooks are designed to serve as study guides for individuals or small discipleship groups of 2-12 (ideal 3-8) committed members. Each of the three studies can be completed in about 12 weekly sessions over one semester or 3-month period with breaks for holidays.

The material in **Course 2** is presented in a somewhat denser writing style and both overlaps and goes beyond that found in Course 1. As such, the course can stand alone and be studied either before or after Course 1 by relatively new believers, long-standing believers, or even members of churches who might not consider themselves to be "evangelical" in their focus or traditional affiliations. New groups may gather and start at any time with motivated leaders who have good reputations in their local churches. Unlike Course 1 which relies on having separate groups for men and women to preserve safe sharing of sensitive personal subjects, **Course 2** content can be handled well by mixed groups.

Each of the three **Course 2** guides is divided into twelve 4-page weekly interactive lessons – four lessons on each of the three Understandings in the first two guides and four lessons on Destination, Transition, and Journey in this, the third and final guide. Supplementary handouts designed to accompany each study guide in the series are available online at www.celebratesalvation.org/more or in a companion book.

Heaven: Our Ultimate Destiny opens up the whole world of promise and imagination associated with our so-called "final state" or eternal inheritance as children of God. In this thought-provoking study in our *Series* we investigate a number of often unexamined aspects of what "heaven" means to us. Where will we be going, what will happen there and along the way, and how can we be preparing now? Search God's Word with us for real hope that He can strengthen into solid faith.

Now faith is the assurance of things hoped for, the conviction of things not seen. For by it the people of old received their commendation. Hebrews 11:1-2

Discipleship Course 2 Design

Course 2 Group Guidelines

1. Prepare for each meeting by reading the week's lesson and writing down some notes about each question in advance.
2. Try to keep your group sharing focused on your own thoughts, feelings, experiences, and insights about each question. Limit your sharing to allow room for group discussion.
3. Please avoid cross-talk. Cross-talk is when two people engage in side conversations during the meeting that exclude others. Each person is free to express their own feelings without interruptions.
4. Remember that we are here to support one another, not to instruct, preach at, or "fix" one another.
5. Anonymity and confidentiality are essential requirements in a trusting discipleship group. Personal information that is shared in the group stays in the group.
6. Offensive or demeaning language has no place in a Christian fellowship group.
7. Please silence your personal electronic devices and put them aside.

Suggestions for Course 2 Group Leadership

Unlike the first two studies in Course 1, mixed groups are acceptable in all Course 2 studies. Schedule regular weekly meetings to last about 90 minutes. Ensure participants have study guides and access to handouts.

1. Gather group in a circle and open meeting on time with prayer and brief comments about group business and upcoming events.
2. Go around circle with introductions including first name in early group meetings, brief status of faith, and personal concerns for prayer.
3. Continue around the circle by sequentially reading the 3 Realms and 7 Understandings and the Group Guidelines for the first few meetings, then one of the Confessional Prayers in unison at every group meeting.
4. Start each lesson by reading the introductory paragraphs around the circle and then opening with the first question.
5. Keep group sharing within Guidelines.
6. Circulate basket for prayer requests; then recirculate so each person who submitted one can take a different one home for intercession.
7. Bring copies of next week's handouts to pass out in advance.
8. Close meeting on time with prayer, allowing members to linger for conversation for a while. Refreshments optional.

Background Material

Confession and Prayer

The 23ʳᵈ Psalm

The LORD is my shepherd; I shall not want. He makes me lie down in green pastures. He leads me beside still waters. He restores my soul. He leads me in paths of righteousness for his name's sake. Even though I walk through the valley of the shadow of death, I will fear no evil, for you are with me; your rod and your staff, they comfort me. You prepare a table before me in the presence of my enemies; you anoint my head with oil; my cup overflows. Surely goodness and mercy shall follow me all the days of my life, and I shall dwell in the house of the LORD forever.

David

The Lord's Prayer

"Our Father in heaven, hallowed be YOUR NAME. Your Kingdom come, Your will be done on earth as it is in heaven. Give us this day our daily bread, and forgive us our sins, as we forgive those who sin against us. Do not lead us into temptation, but deliver us from the evil one, for Yours is the Kingdom and the power and the glory forever. Amen."

Jesus

The Serenity Prayer

God, grant me the serenity to accept the things I cannot change, the courage to change the things I can, and the wisdom to know the difference. Living one day at a time, enjoying one moment at a time; accepting hardship as a pathway to peace; taking, as Jesus did, this sinful world as it is, not as I would have it; trusting that You will make all things right if I surrender to Your will; so that I may be reasonably happy in this life and supremely happy with You forever in the next. Amen.

Reinhold Niebuhr

Our ultimate hope?

What is an "ultimate" reality? Is it something that's so far out there that it's over the top? Is it the kind of thing we can only dream about or try to imagine in our minds and do our best to grasp but that always seems just out of our reach? Should we be joining Judy Garland in singing

> Somewhere over the rainbow, way up high
> There's a land that I heard of once in a lullaby…

Perhaps we didn't hear about the "heaven" that we have in our hearts – the ultimate reward that we're hoping for – "in a lullaby" but it comes to mind when we read many passages in the Bible like this one:

Blessed be the God and Father of our Lord Jesus Christ! According to his great mercy, he has caused us to be born again to a living hope through the resurrection of Jesus Christ from the dead, to an inheritance that is imperishable, undefiled, and unfading, kept in heaven for you, who by God's power are being guarded through faith for a salvation ready to be revealed in the last time. 1 Peter 1:3-5

But is spending eternity in "heaven" after we die our ultimate hope? Is our hope in a place or a destination? No, it's even deeper and more solid than that – our ultimate hope is in God and His Word:

And now, O LORD, for what do I wait? My hope is in you. Psalm 39:7
You are my hiding place and my shield; I hope in your word. Psalm 119:114
I wait for the LORD, my soul waits, and in his word I hope. Psalm 130:5

God's Word tells us that godly hope is one of three interrelated gifts in life that remain and abide in Him, all bound together in the divine *agape* love of the triune Godhead as outlined below:

Faith, **hope**, *and* **love** *abide, these three, but the greatest of these is* **love**.
1 Corinthians 13:13

For **God** *so* **loved** *the world, that he gave his only* **Son**… "I am the way, and the truth, and the life. No one comes to the* **Father** *except through me.* John 3:16; 14:6

And the **Father**… *shall give you another* **Comforter** *that he may be with you forever.* John 14:16

Son
Door
Way
Truth
Life

Faith

Hope

Holy Spirit
Insight, Wisdom
Understanding

Love

Father
Attachment
Commitment

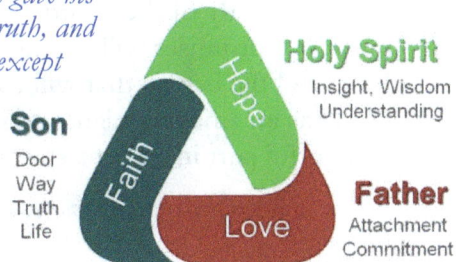

Heaven: Our Ultimate Destiny

Take a good look at the harmony and synergy and eternal "oneness" of our God! The Father sends His Son and gives the Son all authority under Him. We accept God's invitation and go through the Door of faith in Christ and are born again as adopted children of God. The Son asks, and the Father sends the Holy Spirit to comfort, guide, and lead us into all truth and to remind us of everything that the Son has said.

All we need to do is put our trust/faith and hope in Him and His love, and our God takes over and works out all the rest with our cooperation. Follow this endless cycle of love around, and you're at home forever! It is finished! As John and Solomon wrote so long ago

I write these things to you who believe in the name of the Son of God, that you may know that you have eternal life.   1 John 5:13

Trust in the LORD with all your heart, and do not lean on your own understanding. In all your ways acknowledge him, and he will make straight your paths.   Proverbs 3:5-6

How much of the future can we accurately predict or imagine? How much clarity can our thinking have about "heaven"? Let's look at the verse that immediately precedes our "*faith, hope, and love abide*" passage:

For now we see in a mirror dimly, but then face to face. Now I know in part; then I shall know fully, even as I have been fully known.   1 Corinthians 13:12

That's pretty clear – we can't put together the whole picture of what "heaven" might be like, partly because God's Word doesn't give us all the details. Can (or should) we even try in the meantime? Of course! As we "*seek first the Kingdom of God and His righteousness*" by getting to know Him and His Word better, more and more things become clear.

1. Access to eternal life is through faith in Jesus (our Door), not a detailed understanding of what "heaven" will be like.
2. Prayerful study of the Word with a focus on God's covenants and prophetic promises will reveal exciting details about the return of Jesus and the events that will follow.
3. God has an amazing plan, and each one of us ultimately has a wonderful part in it. Let's start digging into His Word together!

In my Father's house are many rooms. If it were not so, would I have told you that I go to prepare a place for you?   John 14:2

Our ultimate hope?

Heaven: Our Ultimate Destiny
F - Living faithful lives into eternity

He has made everything beautiful in its time. Also, he has put eternity into man's heart, yet so that he cannot find out [or understand completely] what God has done from the beginning to the end.　　　Ecclesiastes 3:11

The Challenges of Death and Eternity

This may be the most difficult study guide in our *Series*. We've all been exposed to the idea of eternal life after death, but it's a hazy idea – a dream of sorts like a fairy tale – that something will happen to us after we die, depending on how we've lived our lives up until then. It might have come from assurances given that a loved one, perhaps a recently deceased grandparent, will be going to Heaven where we will see them again. We may have heard about the promise of eternal life in Heaven with God for "good people" or those who have put their trust in Jesus.

The topic brings up images of floating around on the clouds or walking streets paved with gold and hearing lovely music being played by angels on harps. Maybe we've heard that we can anticipate seeing historical figures or asking God lots of questions and being encouraged by His responses. It's all supposed to sound very delightful, but some of us may wonder if a "Heaven" like this won't be boring compared with our current lives and favorite entertainments, behaviors, and friends.

Then there are the troubling alternatives that present themselves. What if we aren't "good enough" to go straight to Heaven but need to go to some kind of painful "reform school" for incompletely sanctified sinners, an "intermediate state" of suffering somewhere between Hell and Heaven where we can get our acts together enough to warrant an uncertain eternity of blessings and rewards? And what if (Heaven forbid!) we should fail there and end up in the eternal torment of Hell? Who goes where and how and when? Besides, if there actually is a place like Hell, would a loving God send anyone there?

These are challenging topics to speculate about but thankfully the Bible, both Old and New Testaments, has a lot to say about them. Many of these Scriptural passages are "so prophetic" that they seem to speak only in allegorical terms of a future we haven't encountered. Extra-biblical accounts have also been written by people who claim to have died and come back to life. Perhaps we should agree with G. K. Chesterton when he observed in his masterpiece of Christian apologetics, *Orthodoxy*, "The poet only asks to get his head into the heavens. It is the logician who seeks to get the heavens into his head. And it is his head that splits."

This is the field of study in our faith that is referred to in two words derived from the Greek, specifically "apocalyptic eschatology." That's quite a mouthful, isn't it? "Apocalyptic" comes from **ἀποκαλύπτειν** (*apokalúptein*, "to reveal or uncover what is hidden"). "Eschatology" comes from **ἔσχατος** (*eskhatos*, "last, final, extreme, best or worst") and **-ολογία** (*-ologia*, "the study of"), meaning that it refers to the branch of theology that studies "last things" with focus on four specific elements of the ultimate destiny of mankind: death, judgment, heaven and hell.

The closing book in our Bible is called "The Apocalypse of John" or the Book of Revelation. Although some rather catastrophic things are discussed in apocalyptic literature, the word actually refers to the process of revealing hidden knowledge to readers. And when we are confronted with troubling or apparently unfulfilled prophetic passages ("revelations"), we often dismiss them with three very natural human responses: *marginalization* (the subject is too confusing to even think about), *postponement* (death or the end is far off in the future, if at all), or *allegorizing* (the Bible describes the end times in figures of speech only).

In other words, instead of praying and studying, we tend to avoid the subject by rationalizing, minimizing, or simply procrastinating our way out. As we wondered in our "Kingdom" study, should we just join Doris Day in singing "Que sera será" (*what will be will be*) with our heads in the soft sand, or will we press in by continuing to ask, seek, and knock as we search God's Word for clearer revelations of His hopes and plans for us?

*Then I saw **a new heaven and a new earth**, for the first heaven and the first earth had passed away, and the sea was no more. And I saw the holy city, **new Jerusalem, coming down out of heaven from God**, prepared as a bride adorned for her husband. And I heard a loud voice from the throne saying, **"Behold, the dwelling place of God is with man**. He will dwell with them, and they will be his people, and God himself will be with them as their God. He will wipe away every tear from their eyes, and death shall be no more, neither shall there be mourning, nor crying, nor pain anymore, for the former things have passed away. And he who was seated on the throne said, **"Behold, I am making all things new."*** Revelation 21:1-5

The Challenges of Death and Eternity

Lesson 1F
Are we predestined?

Understanding 7: Our eternal home – Destination. Casting a vision of where we will be after we die and how we can live our lives between now and then.

How knowing the difference between "destiny" and "destination" can have a clarifying effect on the hopes and expectations we carry for our lives after death.

Destiny is that to which any person is destined; a predetermined state; a condition foreordained by the Divine, while **destination** is the ultimate place set for the end of a journey, or to which something is sent; a place or point aimed at. Both of these terms assume the passage of time and carry with them some sense of space or place in our universe. But what about eternity and the "heaven of heavens" where God dwells, which are beyond the created universe of time and space that we know?

The first challenge we encounter is time. When God identified Himself to Moses as "I AM" He revealed that He simply is, was, and always will be. God has profound feelings but nothing catches Him by surprise. He is the Alpha and the Omega, the beginning and the end, and is in touch with any and every moment in time. Consider God's questions for Job:

Where were you when I laid the foundation of the earth? Tell me, if you have understanding. Who determined its measurements – surely you know! Or who stretched the line upon it? On what were its bases sunk, or who laid its cornerstone, when the morning stars sang together and all the sons of God shouted for joy?
Job 38:1-7

Let's face it joyfully: our destiny is in God's hands alone! The God who knew who Moses was knows our beginnings, our end, and all our thoughts and actions in between – and He still loves us! Those of us who have placed our trust in our Lord and Savior are predestined to share in His glory and inheritance. It is finished!

For those whom he foreknew he also predestined to be conformed to the image of his Son, in order that he might be the firstborn among many brothers. And those

Heaven: Our Ultimate Destiny

whom he predestined he also called, and those whom he called he also justified, and those whom he justified he also glorified.   Romans 8:29-30

Please don't get tangled up in trying to figure out how God is able to reconcile predestination with His gift to us of free will. Trust Him – He has had it all figured out for a long, long time. What remains for us to discern and decide is what we think our ultimate destiny is and what we're being called to do with our lives between now and then.

Why try to discern something as challenging as our future? Let's think of it this way. If you and your family are planning to go on a trip, isn't it helpful to have an idea about where you're going, your route, and what you might do to pack and prepare for that? Maybe you'd like to study a bit about your destination and what you might hope to be doing there.

What? Will we be going to "heaven" and doing things, each one of us with our unique identities, gifts, and personalities? Well, the Bible doesn't suggest that we'll pass through death and be resurrected to new life as someone else. Healed, cleansed, and perfected, yes, but we already became "*new creations*" when we gave our lives to Christ.

Will we also have people to see, places to go, and meaningful things to do? Brothers and sisters, we'll be graduating into the fulfillment of God's Kingdom and eternity, not retiring from human life. The "*new heavens and new earth*" that we're headed for are going to be amazingly engaging. After all, we've been created as human beings with purpose and are going to be spending eternity there, so we shouldn't be looking forward to lying around aimlessly and being bored. God's got plans for each one of us that have been designed specifically with us in mind since the foundations of the world.

The mental bridge we need to cross now has to do with the promised Second Coming of Jesus when He returns to establish His Millennial Kingdom on earth. This is neither the end of time nor yet the beginning of the *new heavens and new earth*. It's a 1,000 year period of living under His loving guidance and protection and rebuilding our current world as the Kingdom of God with the devil's power bound. Can you imagine that? Let's look at what Jesus read when He began His ministry in Galilee:

The Spirit of the Lord God is upon me, because the Lord has anointed me to bring good news to the poor; he has sent me to bind up the brokenhearted, to proclaim liberty to the captives, and the opening of the prison to those who are bound; to proclaim the year of the Lord's favor, † *and the day of vengeance of our God; to comfort all who mourn; to grant to those who mourn in Zion — to give them a beautiful headdress instead of ashes, the oil of gladness instead of mourning, the garment of praise instead of a faint spirit; that they may be called oaks of righteousness, the planting of the Lord, that he may be glorified. They shall build up the ancient ruins; they shall raise up the former devastations; they shall repair the ruined cities, the devastations of many generations.*   Isaiah 61:1-4

Jesus stopped at the cross mark † above and said, *"Today this Scripture has been fulfilled in your hearing."* We can be assured that the rest of this passage will come to pass when He returns. Where will we be then?

For the Lord himself will descend from heaven with a cry of command, with the voice of an archangel, and with the sound of the trumpet of God. And the dead in Christ will rise first. Then we who are alive, who are left, will be caught up together with them in the clouds to meet the Lord in the air, and so we will always be with the Lord.   1 Thessalonians 4:16-17

Yes, when we die we'll emerge in our resurrected bodies to meet Jesus in the first heaven as He returns (Zech. 14) to establish His Millennial Kingdom with our help in the rebuilding. This is excitingly good news!

Appreciating our Destiny

1. Have you ever thought about how much God knows about you and loves you? When did you first meet Him?

2. When you first became a believer, did you have any awareness of God's presence and calling on your life?

Heaven: Our Ultimate Destiny

14

3. Do you have any direct experiences of God's faithfulness to you or your family that you'd like to share?

4. Do you have any concerns about your calling and election to receive eternal life?

5. What are you currently looking forward to or hoping for after you die?

As you go through this study you might take advantage of some handouts from our Kingdom study like: **New Testament Eschatology**, **Prophetic Views of the Millennium**, **Bible Bookends**, **Millennial Scripture Verses**, and **The Millennial Kingdom and the Eternal State**, all available under "Kingdom" at https://www.celebratesalvation.org/more/#2):

Lesson 2F
Where is Heaven?

Understanding 7: Our eternal home – Destination. Casting a vision of where we will be after we die and how we can live our lives between now and then.

Continued examination of our thoughts and meditations when we contemplate Heaven in the light of Scripture and where it might be located in space and time.

It might come as a surprise to many in today's Christian community that the idea of "Heaven," as many of us are accustomed to imagine it, does not come directly from either the Old or New Testament prophetic writings in our Bibles. Much of it, in fact, comes from ancient pagan mythologies and the speculations of Greek philosophers and Hebrew mystics, all dressed up in figurative literature and art.

Let's set aside many of our notions as we begin and spend some time together studying the Word of God more closely. What are the Scriptures speaking about when they mention "heaven"?

Heaven: Our Ultimate Destiny

16

Fortunately, there are essentially only two words that are consistently used throughout the Bible that are translated either as "heaven" or "the heavens" – Hebrew שָׁמַיִם (*shamayim*) and Greek οὐρανός (*ouranos*). Both of these words are literally plural and refer generically to the three overlapping realms that surround the earth:

1. the atmosphere where clouds and weather occur and birds fly
2. outer space where the heavenly bodies are arrayed
3. beyond our sight where God dwells in eternity

Scripture distinguishes between the different realms of "the heavens" through their context or the addition of further descriptors, resulting in translations like "visible sky" or "skies" which may include 1 or 2 and simply "heaven" (singular) or "heaven of heavens" which may refer to "the third heaven" that Paul mentioned in 2 Corinthians 12:2:

> *I know a man in Christ who fourteen years ago was caught up to the third heaven – whether in the body or out of the body I do not know, God knows.*

But how can we human beings wrap our minds around the idea of eternity, much less what the "heaven of heavens" beyond time and space must be like? Where was God when He created the universe?

Well, there's an interesting revelation that occurs throughout the Bible. God's plan may differ somewhat from what we've been imagining. If He is to be taken at His Word, it appears that our God intends to bring the perfection of His full plan for the created universe into being by "making all things new" in the form of "a new heaven and a new earth" and then furnishing this new earth with a "new Jerusalem" which He has designed in the heaven of heavens where He dwells for us to live in perfect harmony with Him on the new earth He's created..

Maybe the place with "rooms" that Jesus has been preparing for each of us in His Father's house, rooms furnished with the "treasures in heaven" we've been laying up, will come "down out of heaven from God" along with the "new Jerusalem" at the close of the age. When? How about after a thousand years of joyful fruitfulness helping build His Millennial Kingdom?

Let's dive into the Word together and see what we find by taking a closer look at a pair of promises Peter shared with us in his second epistle, the first being God's promise of a "*new heavens and earth*":

But according to his promise we are waiting for new heavens and a new earth in which righteousness dwells.   2 Peter 3:13

The Greek word used in this context for "*new*" is **καινός** (*kainos*), which means fresh, renewed, or new in quality. What we think of as something brand-new or new in time is usually designated by the Greek word **νέος** (*neos*). *Kainos* takes something valuable and dramatically transforms it. *Neos* starts over from scratch with a full replacement.

The second promise is that the "*new heavens and new earth*" will culminate in a society established by Jesus during His Millennial reign where "*righteousness dwells*" as Isaiah prophesied. Clearly, this will be a place where people are in ideal relationships with God, others, and the world around them. Arriving at a completely renewed and sinless world will require a divinely penetrating and thorough process of purification, likened in many verses to a cleansing fire. Are we ready?

Who can endure the day of his coming, and who can stand when he appears? For he is like a refiner's fire and like fullers' soap. He will sit as a refiner and purifier of silver, and he will purify the sons of Levi and refine them like gold and silver, and they will bring offerings in righteousness to the LORD.   Malachi 3:2-3

Awakening to God's eternal dream

1. Let your thoughts wander prayerfully. What would a renewed "heaven on earth" look like to you?

2. The dream Martin Luther King, Jr. had sounds a lot like the Millennial Kingdom. Can we dream beyond that into infinity?

Heaven: Our Ultimate Destiny

3. When you pray "*Your Kingdom come, Your will be done on earth as it is in heaven*" what other thoughts and imaginations come to mind?

4. Can you recall any other prophetic Scripture passages that describe God's promises about our inheritance in "heaven"? List a few.

5. What images of a transformed earth and skies do the Scriptures use to describe what our eternal state will be like beyond the Millennium?

For more depth on this subject, see our two handouts on this topic **Translation of *Ouranos*** and **Three Realms of the Heavens** available at https://www.celebratesalvation.org/more/#2.

Lesson 3F
What will Heaven be like?

Understanding 7: Our eternal home – Destination. Casting a vision of where we will be after we die and how we can live our lives between now and then.

Searching the Word of God for insights about what our circumstances and surroundings will resemble when we arrive at and live in our eternal state.

Imagination

How do we envision the future? Only through exercising our God-given ability to imagine, a remarkable human capacity that allows us to hope, plan, have trust and faith in, and make decisions based on realities like the future that we can't see in any other way. So can we "only imagine" what the circumstances of our lives might be like in the future (and specifically after we die) or can we find out more in advance? There are two approaches: we can base our imaginary thoughts on unverified experiences, myths, and fables or on another much more reliable source, the Word of God.

Fortunately, it turns out that the Bible actually has a lot to say about the future and the particulars of life after death. In fact, there are a great many portions of the Bible that contain as yet unfulfilled prophecies about the future, including promises and descriptions of what our lives will be like after we die. Keeping what Paul wrote in 1 Corinthians 13:12 (*Now I know in part; then I shall know fully, even as I have been fully known*) in mind, let's take a closer look at a number of Biblical passages that relate to several aspects of this critical topic.

Where will we be?

Both Old and New Testaments contain a remarkable number of detailed passages that talk about what we will face together at the Second Coming of Christ and beyond, many of which we have already looked at fairly closely in our previous Kingdom study. Some of the best and most consistent summary passages are found in Chapters 65 and 66 of Isaiah as well as 20 and 21 at the end of the Book of Revelation (see **End Times Scripture References** handout).

Heaven: Our Ultimate Destiny

The Scriptures agree that life here on earth will be more afflicted with strife ("tribulation") as the Lord's return approaches, and then rescued by His dramatic arrival "on the clouds" accompanied by both living and resurrected saints. The witness of the Bible is that He will alight on the Mount of Olives and establish the seat of His earthly reign in Jerusalem. We will then dwell with Him in a restored and transformed world immersed (baptized) in a spiritually pure atmosphere and filled with every ideal provision for living harmonious, long, and fruitful lives.

For the earth will be filled with the knowledge of the glory of the LORD as the waters cover the sea.   Habakkuk 2:14

What will our bodies and souls be like?

As Paul describes in 1 Corinthians 15, the entire promise of our personal resurrection is based on the demonstrated resurrection of Jesus. The Word indicates that we will be miraculously reconstituted bodily in a purified, healthy, and ideal form (fearfully and wonderfully remade in His Image), with our souls cleansed of and freed from all the ravages of sickness and sin and able to demonstrate the full fruit of the Spirit. Like Jesus we will be recognizable to each other in the glorified form that God designed us to inhabit with all of its divine capabilities.

How will we communicate with one another?

God's work is, from Alpha to Omega, always quite miraculous. Ponder this observation for a while. On the day of Pentecost, Acts reports:

They were all filled with the Holy Spirit and began to speak in other tongues as the Spirit gave them utterance. Now there were dwelling in Jerusalem Jews, devout men from every nation under heaven… and they were amazed and astonished, saying, "Are not all these who are speaking Galileans? And how is it that we hear, each of us in his own native language?   Acts 2:4-8

We tend to think of the gift of tongues as a somewhat odd, pointless, and sensational sign. But what if the gifts of the Spirit listed in 1 Corinthians 12 have been given to us as a mere foretaste of God's purposes in the fullness of time? We will certainly need the ability to understand and communicate freely with people from all ages and tongues when He gathers His people as Zephaniah foretold.

For then I will restore to the peoples a pure language that they all may call on the name of the LORD, to serve Him with one accord.   Zephaniah 3:9

What will our relationships and mobility be like?

By God's grace we'll be able to find, recognize, and communicate joyfully and in pure harmony with the Lord, all the saints we've known in our lives, and all those throughout history that we'll get to know. In the light of eternity time will be no obstacle. But what about everything else that will need to be taken care of, like getting around? As one example, let's take a look at the report of Philip and the eunuch in Acts:

And... they both went down into the water, Philip and the eunuch, and he baptized him. And when they came up out of the water, the Spirit of the Lord carried Philip away... but Philip found himself at Azotus, and as he passed through he preached the gospel to all the towns... Acts 8:38-40

The Greek root word that describes Philip being "carried away" is the same ἁρπάζω (*harpazó*) used by Paul to note how we all will be "caught up" and transported to join Christ at His Second Coming:

And the dead in Christ will rise first. Then we who are alive, who are left, will be caught up together with them in the clouds to meet the Lord in the air, and so we will always be with the Lord. 1 Thessalonians 4:16-17

What God wants and wills for us in keeping with the Lord's Prayer will surely come about in His wonderfully miraculous timing and way.

Awakening to the Age to Come

1. Write down some of your imaginations about heaven up until now. Then try to identify Scripture references that support each one.

2. Have you been able to envision a timeline that includes Christ's Second Coming, Millennial Reign, Judgment, and a New Earth?

Heaven: Our Ultimate Destiny

3. Is the idea that our ultimate destiny may be a divinely recreated paradise difficult for you to take hold of? In what ways?

4. What are some of your deepest hopes about what eternal life with God will be like? List some Bible verses that confirm them.

5. Review the gifts of the Spirit listed in 1 Corinthians 12:4-11 and list those you have begun to receive. Are you learning to exercise them?

Please review our handouts on **Heaven in a Biblical Perspective**, **Heavenly Imaginations,** and **End Times Scripture References** available online at https://www.celebratesalvation.org/more/#2.

Understanding 7: Destination   Lesson 3F

Lesson 4F
Will everyone go to Heaven?

Understanding 7: Our eternal home – Destination. Casting a vision of where we will be after we die and how we can live our lives between now and then.

Taking a careful look at what Scripture reveals about final judgment and our calling to prepare ourselves and others for it.

Just as it is appointed for man to die once, and after that comes judgment, so Christ, having been offered once to bear the sins of many, will appear a second time, not to deal with sin but to save those who are eagerly waiting for him.

Hebrews 9:27-28

This would be a good time to read Christ's Olivet Discourse in Matthew 24-25 (also in Mark 13 and Luke 21) again. Although an entire assortment of theoretical possibilities have been proposed over the millennia, especially by other religions and sects, Jesus' teachings and the Biblical record are clear from beginning to end that we will all face a final judgment when we die with two and only two outcomes: a breathtaking eternity with God in His Kingdom ("heaven") or a miserable eternity of isolation apart from the grace of God in "hell."

The most prominent alternatives to this reality in today's secular and alternative faith worlds include variants of "annihilationism" (we just dissolve when we die and are gone), "universalism" (we all end up in bliss), "reincarnation" (we move through endless cycles and levels of rebirth), and other mixed outcomes and opportunities of reward and punishment found in Catholic, Islamic, and Mormon formulations.

However, back in the 17th Century a child prodigy, mathematician, philosopher, physicist, and theologian, Blaise Pascal, developed a famous theological argument that became known as "Pascal's wager" which is well worth considering in today's multicultural post-Christian world of free-thinking. As described by Wikipedia, "Pascal argues that a rational person should live as though God exists and seek to believe in God. If God does not exist, such a person will have only a finite loss (some pleasures, luxury, etc.), whereas if God does exist, they stand to

Heaven: Our Ultimate Destiny

receive infinite gains (as represented by eternity in Heaven) and avoid infinite losses (an eternity in Hell)."

Perhaps the argument we're most familiar with is the secular/Unitarian Universalist position that Jesus came as a good man whose primary message was that since God (if there is one worth paying attention to) is a god of perfect Love, everyone will be saved for eternity because a God of Love could never consign a person to an eternity of torment. Let's look at this argument briefly:

First, secularists and Unitarians deny many specifics of divinity, including the divinity of Jesus. In so doing, they have vaguely generalized the characteristics of a God they don't know personally themselves, reducing this "god" to their own version of love, which has become widely confused with natural human passion (*eros*) in the phrase "love is love is love." The main problem here is that God's love (*agape*) goes far deeper than undisciplined *eros* to include a host of compatible and divinely perfected traits like mercy, purity, faithfulness, and justice, all of which are needed to initiate and sustain godly and wholesome relationships. Leaving these out is short-sighted at best. Let's see what Peter's exhortation has to add in the following passage:

His divine power has granted to us all things that pertain to life and godliness, through the knowledge of him who called us to his own glory and excellence, by which he has granted to us his precious and very great promises, so that through them you may become partakers of the divine nature, having escaped from the corruption that is in the world because of sinful desire. For this very reason, make every effort to supplement your faith with virtue, and virtue with knowledge, and knowledge with self-control, and self-control with steadfastness, and steadfastness with godliness, and godliness with brotherly affection, and brotherly affection with love. For if these qualities are yours and are increasing, they keep you from being ineffective or unfruitful in the knowledge of our Lord Jesus Christ. For whoever lacks these qualities is so nearsighted that he is blind, having forgotten that he was cleansed from his former sins. Therefore, brothers, be all the more diligent to confirm your calling and election, for if you practice these qualities you will never fall. For in this way there will be richly provided for you an entrance into the eternal kingdom of our Lord and Savior Jesus Christ. 2 Peter 1:3-11

Our God is Holy, sinless, and pure and He desires us to be transformed by His power into His likeness that we might be prepared and compatible with His plans for our lives together in eternity. He desires to plant perennials in His renewed Garden of Eden, not weeds. He wants adopted sons and daughters who hear and follow his voice and desire to live apart from the serpent who corrupted Adam and Eve. Yes, eternity is waiting patiently for all who will seek God's heart.

For thus says the One who is high and lifted up, who inhabits eternity, whose name is Holy: "I dwell in the high and holy place, and also with him who is of a contrite and lowly spirit, to revive the spirit of the lowly, and to revive the heart of the contrite.   Isaiah 57:15

For if the dead are not raised, not even Christ has been raised. And if Christ has not been raised, your faith is futile and you are still in your sins. Then those also who have fallen asleep in Christ have perished. If in Christ we have hope in this life only, we are of all people most to be pitied.   1 Corinthians 15:16-19

I write these things to you who believe in the name of the Son of God, that you may know that you have eternal life.   1 John 5:13

Awakening to Judgment

1. What thoughts do you have about God's stated plans for final judgment? Is He patient enough with sinners like us?

2. What areas in your life is God trying to reach and redeem right now? Does it matter how you respond?

Heaven: Our Ultimate Destiny

26

3. Do you think God "grades on a curve" and that most people will get a passing grade into heaven based on their own goodness?

4. Is it possible that *"many are called but few are chosen"* and that actually only a small percentage of people will make it to heaven?

5. What difference would it make in your approach to others if you believed that either 1) almost everyone or 2) actually very few were likely to go to heaven?

For an introduction to some non-Christian ideas, read our handouts on **Three Heavenly Mormon Kingdoms** and **Alternative Views of the Afterlife**, available at https://www.celebratesalvation.org/more/#2.

Lesson 5F
What happens when we die?

Understanding 7: Our eternal home – Transition. Casting a vision of where we will be after we die and how we can live our lives between now and then.

Discussing what we may anticipate experiencing when we pass out of mortal life in this world and on to eternal life in the world to come.

To begin gaining an understanding of death and resurrection, we need to contemplate the virtually incredible difference between our amazing Creator God who dwells in eternity and us, as mortal human beings created by Him in His Image. How can we possibly be compared with Him? Well, He's infinite, all-knowing and all powerful. He's the Alpha and the Omega, the Beginning and the End. He created, sustains, and knows all things, and by Him all things hold together. You can continue pondering how great our God is by reading our Handout on **Eternity, Infinity, and God** at https://www.celebratesalvation.org/more/#2.

What about us? We're finite; our lives have a beginning and an end. We remember some things and essentially forget everything else. We do some things right and mess much of the rest up. Sometimes it's hard to say just what it is that we hold together. We each have "*inward parts*" and a "*frame*" (natural body) that David tells us in Psalm 139:13-16 were "*fearfully and wonderfully made*" when we were being "*knitted together in our mothers' wombs.*" But to gain an even broader biblical perspective of how intimately God knows and relates to us, take a break now to read and meditate on all 24 verses of Psalm 139, then return as we examine our human condition in more detail.

According to both testaments of the Bible, human beings are tripartite creatures, meaning that we are composed of three interwoven aspects, a body (or *soma*), a soul (or *psyche*), and a spirit (or *pneuma*). Descriptively, we each have a physical or bodily nature, a psychological dimension or soul where feelings, memory, and rational thought predominate, and a unique spiritual identity or spirit of self-awareness that is able to discern

Heaven: Our Ultimate Destiny

the content and origin of our thoughts, examine the condition of our souls, and consciously communicate with God and others. How can we distinguish among these three aspects? The Word of God provides keys:

Then the Lord God formed the man of dust from the ground and breathed into his nostrils the breath of life, and the man became a living creature. Genesis 2:7

Why are you cast down, O my soul, and why are you in turmoil within me? Hope in God; for I shall again praise him, my salvation. Psalm 42:5

For the word of God is living and active, sharper than any two-edged sword, piercing to the division of soul and of spirit, of joints and of marrow, and discerning the thoughts and intentions of the heart. Hebrews 4:12

Now may the God of peace himself sanctify you completely, and may your whole spirit and soul and body be kept blameless at the coming of our Lord Jesus Christ. 1 Thessalonians 5:23

And do not fear those who kill the body but cannot kill the soul. Rather fear him who can destroy both soul and body in hell. Matthew 10:28

One might think that when our bodies die, all our abilities to feel and think and identify ourselves would be lost. We wonder what becomes of our senses of self and identity, all the relationships and experiences we've had, and our memories and understandings once our spirits have left our mortal bodies and we die. Well, God has ordained that all the data that's been stored in our bodies in the form of our original DNA as well as any record of changes and life experiences that have been stored organically in our brains and tissues has been preserved by our Creator in His "cloud storage" in Heaven. In fact, we might consider one of God's attributes to be that He *is* the "cloud"*!* All He needs to do to resurrect us in His Image is to perform a final clean-up of the "backup" data He's so carefully collected and use this redeemed and sanctified version to "make all things new" in recreating us for our promised eternal life on the other side of death. Can you imagine this?

Back to the question of where will we find ourselves after we die. Will we arrive in some kind of "intermediate state"? We'll be looking more closely at this question in our next two Lessons, but before then let's abandon the fanciful fable about "meeting St. Peter at the pearly gates" and begin to consider a more biblical scenario – that we pass directly through a "time window" in eternity and are ushered into the presence of the Lord in our gloriously resurrected bodies with their completely redeemed and sanctified souls. Paul relates in 1 Corinthians 15 and 1 Thessalonians 4 that Christ's Second Coming or Parousia will all happen *in a moment, in the twinkling of an eye,* and we'll find ourselves joyfully joining Jesus, along with all the past, present, and future saints, as He returns on the clouds to establish His Millennial Kingdom here on earth.

> When Christ shall come with shouts of acclamation,
> to take me home, what joy will fill my heart!
> Then I will bow in humble adoration,
> and there proclaim, my God, how great thou art!
> Chorus:
> Then sings my soul, my Savior God, to thee:
> how great thou art! How great thou art! *

As the Apostle Paul proclaimed in 1 Corinthians 13:12:

> *For now we see in a mirror dimly, but then face to face. Now I know in part; then I shall know fully, even as I have been fully known.*

Passing through death into the afterlife

1. What thoughts cross your mind when you think about the vast complexity of God's creation and the miracle of resurrection?

2. Do you find that your imagination has been occupied by myths about heaven, hell, judgment, and the afterlife? Where are you now?

Heaven: Our Ultimate Destiny

3. What questions do you still have? Write down a list below and seek progressively more reliable understandings from the Scriptures.

4. Is there any limit to what our God can do? What would be changed in your life by being completely redeemed, sanctified, and glorified?

5. Let your mind wander in prayer as you meditate on forgiveness, death, and resurrection and make a list of your hopes and dreams.

For more about this Lesson's topic, reread 1 Corinthians 15 as well as our **Biblical Timetable and Bookends** and **Eternity, Infinity, and God** handouts online at https://www.celebratesalvation.org/more/#2.

* *"How Great Thou Art"*: https://www.youtube.com/watch?v=p-hvI1nbS80

Lesson 6F
Is there an "intermediate state"?

Understanding 7: Our eternal home – Transition. Casting a vision of where we will be after we die and how we can live our lives between now and then.

Comparing the idea of going through an "intermediate state" of continued soul cleansing in the afterlife with Biblical teachings and those of other religions.

While he was in prison for sharing the Gospel Paul wrote a letter to believers in the congregation he had founded earlier in Philippi during his second missionary journey. Being in danger of execution, he wished to encourage the believers of their mutual confidence in Christ.

> *I am sure of this, that he who began a good work in you will bring it to completion at the day of Jesus Christ… For to me to live is Christ, and to die is gain. If I am to live in the flesh, that means fruitful labor for me. Yet which I shall choose I cannot tell. I am hard pressed between the two. My desire is to depart and be with Christ, for that is far better.* Philippians 1:5, 21-23

In this passage Paul references two realities: 1) that Christ will complete the "*good work*" of redemption He began in each believer "*at the day of Jesus Christ*" (i.e., by the time He returns), and 2) that he, Paul, is eagerly looking forward to that "*day.*" But what happens between the time we die and Christ's return, a time referred to in theological circles as "the intermediate state"? Where will we be, and what condition will we be in while we are waiting, so to speak, for His return? Will we go directly to meet the Lord or exist in some fashion between earth and our final destination to undergo further cleansing or discipline? And what about those who haven't put their faith in Christ? What path will they travel?

Since we're all still such a tainted mixture of good and bad, it's natural to wonder about God's plan for dealing with our imperfections in preparation for encountering Him in His perfection when we die.

A major development that took hold in the medieval Catholic Church was the idea and doctrine of Purgatory, which is described in the

Roman Catechism (Part One, Chapter Three, Article 12, Section III, Paragraphs 1030-32) in these words: "All who die in God's grace and friendship, but still imperfectly purified, are indeed assured of their eternal salvation; but after death they undergo purification, so as to achieve the holiness necessary to enter the joy of heaven." Along with this teaching have come vivid descriptions of burning fires, suffering, and torment similar to those depicted by Dante in his *Divine Comedy* that have timelessly captivated the imaginations of many. Partial remedies in the form of prayers for the dead and sacrifices or "indulgences" on their behalf are included in the teaching (see our handout on **Purgatory and Paradise**).

Other Eastern and Western religious traditions, including Jewish, Orthodox, Protestant, Islamic, Buddhist, Taoist, and indigenous myths, also deal with the subject in varying ways. Modern "more enlightened" approaches tend to dismiss the whole subject with the rationale that if there really is a "loving" God or an afterlife, we'll all make it scot-free.

There are at least three big problems with many of these "intermediate state" speculations:

1. They aren't supported by reliable biblical references, the teachings of Jesus, or the witness of the Spirit.
2. They don't deal with the profound difference between the dimensions of time/space and those of eternity
3. They don't address issues of ultimate justice or the condition and fate of "the lost"

But as it is, he has appeared once for all at the end of the ages to put away sin by the sacrifice of himself. And just as it is appointed for man to die once, and after that comes judgment, so Christ, having been offered once to bear the sins of many, will appear a second time, not to deal with sin but to save those who are eagerly waiting for him. Hebrews 9:26-28

And He [Jesus] said to him [the thief beside Him on the cross], "Truly, I say to you, today you will be with me in paradise." Luke 23:43

Arguments in favor of an "intermediate state" assume that the dead depart from life as we know it but not entirely from space and their current place in the passage of time. This means that they would exist and be occupied in some extracorporeal way (with fire?) while waiting beyond "*today*" for the Lord's return, resurrection, and final judgment.

"Enlightenment" ideas like universalism and total annihilation, as noted in Lesson 4, deny the possibility of ultimate justice with appropriate (by whose standards?) rewards and punishments to be reckoned with.

All of this begs the question that is raised by Jesus' call to every human being to be convicted of sin, repent, accept Him as their Lord and Savior, and receive eternal life – namely, what does He save us from? The very essence of Christ's offer of eternal salvation is that we don't have to pay for our own redemption, either before or after we die but will enjoy our "intermediate stage" reigning with Him in the Millennium:

They will be priests of God and of Christ, and they will reign with him for a thousand years. And when the thousand years are ended, Satan will be released from his prison and will come out to deceive the nations that are at the four corners of the earth, Gog and Magog, to gather them for battle; their number is like the sand of the sea. And they marched up over the broad plain of the earth and surrounded the camp of the saints and the beloved city, but fire came down from heaven and consumed them, and the devil who had deceived them was thrown into the lake of fire and sulfur where the beast and the false prophet were, and they will be tormented day and night forever and ever.

Revelation 20:6-10

Your thoughts about an "intermediate stage"

1. What have you been imagining might happen to you and others when you die? Where might you be?

2. Does the idea of Purgatory conjure up any images in your mind? Where do these come from?

Heaven: Our Ultimate Destiny

34

3. Have you engaged in Bible study about the end times and God's Millennial Kingdom? What thoughts come to mind?

4. A lot of organizing and public activity in recent years has put "pride" forward as an antidote to shame. What do you think?

5. How much of your sin, guilt, and shame did Jesus take care of when He died on the cross and rose again? Is more suffering needed?

Be sure you make time to read our handout **Purgatory and Paradise**, available online at https://www.celebratesalvation.org/more/#2.

Lesson 7F
What about the Millennial Kingdom?

Understanding 7: Our eternal home – Transition. Casting a vision of where we will be after we die and how we can live our lives between now and then.

Identifying who will be present to establish and enjoy the Millennial Kingdom with Christ when He returns at His Second Coming.

When the Scriptures consisted only of the Tenakh (what we refer to as the "Old Testament") the people of Israel were looking forward to a Messiah who would rescue them from their bondage under the ungodly and oppressive authorities of this world. As they read the prophetic words they were puzzled by some passages that seemed to indicate the coming of a "suffering servant" who would be "pierced" and "die" like the one foreseen in Isaiah 53 and Zechariah 12. The Messiah they were more eagerly anticipating was a conquering king who would vanquish His enemies and establish Israel as a free and exemplary nation.

When Jesus came in lowliness and humility, they were outraged at claims that He could be the Messiah they were awaiting, and in their frustration and anger they fulfilled their own prophetic word and persecuted, pierced, and put Him to a shameful death by crucifixion.

However, Jesus spoke at various times and places about what would happen to Him, including promises that He would return again as a victorious King during a future time of profound tribulation in the world. Some of His most notable teachings on this subject can be found in Matthew 23-25 in His **Discourse on the End Times**.

The return of Christ is divinely linked with His departure in Acts 1:6-10:

So when they had come together, they asked him, "Lord, will you at this time restore the kingdom to Israel?" He said to them, "It is not for you to know times or seasons that the Father has fixed by his own authority. But you will receive power when the Holy Spirit has come upon you, and you will be my witnesses in Jerusalem and in all Judea and Samaria, and to the end of the earth." And

Heaven: Our Ultimate Destiny

when he had said these things, as they were looking on, he was lifted up, and a cloud took him out of their sight. And while they were gazing into heaven as he went, behold, two men [angels] stood by them in white robes, and said, "Men of Galilee, why do you stand looking into heaven? This Jesus, who was taken up from you into heaven, will come in the same way as you saw him go into heaven."

In other words, Jesus will descend from Heaven and return to the earth in bodily form, arriving on the Mount of Olives and coming to nearby Jerusalem to "*restore the kingdom to Israel*" in fulfillment of the prayer He taught His disciples to use as a model in which we petition the Father to "*let your kingdom come, your will be done, on earth as it is in heaven.*" Whose kingdom? God's. Where? On earth in fulfillment of Isaiah 61.

When will this earthly Kingdom of God come and how long will it last? Well, it started to arrive in the hearts of believers as soon as they began hearing and yielding to the message of Christ, and its influence has been spreading far and wide since then. However, its full establishment won't come until Christ has returned in victory, putting His enemies to flight and banishing His adversary, Satan, from the earth. Placed in time and space, this sequence of events can only refer to the Millennial Kingdom spoken of so clearly in Revelation 19 and 20 where the "*one thousand year*" duration is unmistakably noted fully five times.

There are many human ideas about the Biblical vision of how the future will unfold, as we've reviewed in our Kingdom study guide and outlined in our handout entitled **Prophetic Views of the Millennium**. Some agree with our "traditional premillennial" view that Christ will return before the Millennium, while others continue to hold an "amillennial" view that sees the Millennial Kingdom as an allegory of the Church. Still others hold a "postmillennial" view that we will be able to establish the Kingdom on our own by spreading the Gospel to the whole world. Hopefully, by the end of our study series we will each be able to arrive at an understanding about the difference our beliefs in these matters can make in our outlook and behavior between now and when we die.

Who will be present when Christ returns at His Second Coming? All of the saints who have put their trust in Him will accompany Him and will be met by those left alive on earth after the horror and ruination of the Great Tribulation and battle of Armageddon. Under Christ's loving guidance the remaining sick and wounded will be ministered to and together they "*shall repair the ruined cities, the devastations of many generations*" as prophesied in Isaiah 61. Only God knows the details about what living in the Millennial Kingdom will be like, but it will be wonderful. Between now and then will all of us have to face "tribulations" of various kinds? "*In this world*" we certainly will, but Jesus has promised to be with us to comfort and guide us "*even to the end of the age.*"

Will there be rewards for faithfulness? Yes, both here and forever! First He rewards us by revealing Himself and making His Word come alive to us. Then He calls and equips us for rewarding tasks to be carried out in His Kingdom, here and in the age to come. And finally He promises that we will be able to enjoy the fruits of our labor along with Him and a host of fellow believers for all eternity, apart from Satan's wiles!

For the grace of God has appeared, bringing salvation for all people, training us to renounce ungodliness and worldly passions, and to live self-controlled, upright, and godly lives in the present age, waiting for our blessed hope, the appearing of the glory of our great God and Savior Jesus Christ, who gave himself for us to redeem us from all lawlessness and to purify for himself a people for his own possession who are zealous for good works.   Titus 2:11-14

Imagining the Millennial Kingdom

1. As you study this Lesson, take note of promises that speak to your heart. What are some of them?

2. In addition to hopes and positive visions, do you have any concerns or fears about inheriting eternal life after death?

Heaven: Our Ultimate Destiny

3. Are you beginning to envision the Millennial Kingdom here on earth as an "intermediate state" between death and Heaven?

4. What would you like to see happen to you or be fulfilled on earth during your time in the Millennial Kingdom?

5. Can you think of any ways you would like the Lord to guide, instruct, or reassure you between now and when you die?

Do some studying before you answer each question by reviewing our handout **Prophetic Views of the Millennium** (linked in our previous Kingdom study list) as well as our handout **Discourse on the End Times**, both online at https://www.celebratesalvation.org/more/#2.

Lesson 8F
When does final judgment occur?

Understanding 7: Our eternal home – Transition. Casting a vision of where we will be after we die and how we can live our lives between now and then.

How judgment differs for believers and unbelievers, both during the tribulations of our current lives and then beyond death into eternity.

The whole concept of judgment brings up the subjects of right and wrong, accusations and defenses, the gathering of evidence, trials and tribulations, verdicts of conviction or acquittal, and ultimately rewards and/or punishments. Who is the accused, and who are their accusers, defense team, and judges?

Over the course of history human beings have been subject to trials and tribulations, ranging from minor frustrations and harassments to major catastrophes like earthquakes, eruptions, wars, famines, pandemic plagues and holocausts, difficulties that test us and our faith or can even break us. The last century has seen some of the worst of these.

When tribulation arises, two questions usually come to mind: why is this happening to me, and what can or should I do about it? The first question has three primary answers: either we made a mistake, or someone else did something wrong, or the tribulation is of a kind where forces beyond anyone's control are operating.

During our lifetimes, we can also all expect to be accused, whether rightly or wrongly, of bad attitudes and misbehaviors that call for correction. Who the judge is, where we place our faith, how we handle ourselves, and who we call upon to defend us are the crucial issues. If we recognize that our errors have had a negative effect on others, we need to seek reconciliation by reaching out to those we've offended with a humble apology, make amends when possible, and seek forgiveness. But what if the primary problem is more diffuse like an earthquake, vague like an accident, or something you've done to

Heaven: Our Ultimate Destiny

yourself like an addiction? Who do you seek to reconcile with then, and what about the damage that's been done?

As unbelievable as it may seem, our infinite, all-knowing God keeps an account of everything that happens in His universe and knows the damage every error has done, large or small. In this regard, we can say that ultimately the errors we make, intentionally and unintentionally, accumulate to the Creator's account. As David, the Psalmist confessed:

Against you, you only, have I sinned and done what is evil in your sight, so that you may be justified in your words and blameless in your judgment. Psalm 51:4

Mercifully, He is ready to review our account, reconcile it with us, and help us recover and make whatever amends are appropriate. He even sends the Holy Spirit to convict us of our sin and turn our hearts to Him for forgiveness and reconciliation. Without His Grace we have no hope: our sins and their negative effects just keep accumulating the older we get, provoking anger and blaming God or others and causing growing breaches in our relationships with our Maker and those around us.

In spite of whatever attempts we make throughout our lives to improve and reconcile with God and those around us, however, we inevitably keep accumulating a residual debt of sin. Some of us have more time and understanding to deal with these things, while others are more careless and limited. Think about the thieves who were crucified with Christ, compared with people you might know who just "always seem to get it right." Jesus knew that all three of them being crucified were about to die, and He said to one thief, "*Today you will be with me in paradise*" a promise that begs at least 4 questions: Where is "*paradise*"? What about the other thief? What about "purgatory"? And you?

The first answer is found in Revelation 2:7 where God tells us that our inheritance will start with a sojourn in a paradise like Eden:

To the one who conquers I will grant to eat of the tree of life, which is in the paradise of God.

Did the other thief still have time to give his heart to Jesus? Yes, we all do until we die. And, when Jesus proclaimed "*It is finished!*" just before he died on the cross, He declared that any threat of purgatory is null and void. So when does our last or <u>final</u> judgment occur? The obvious answer is that it will happen to each one of us when we die:

And just as it is appointed for man to die once, and after that comes judgment, so Christ, having been offered once to bear the sins of many, will appear a second time, not to deal with sin but to save those who are eagerly waiting for him.

Hebrews 9:27-28

However, since some of us may still be alive in Christ when He returns as noted above, the rewards of our faithfulness will begin to manifest when, as Paul tells us in 1 Thessalonians 4:17, we join the saints with Jesus "*in the clouds*" upon His return to establish the Millennial Kingdom. Only at the close of the Millennium will the historical final judgment of the ages come to pass as described in Revelation 20 and 21:

And when the thousand years are ended… Then I saw a great white throne and him who was seated on it. From his presence earth and sky fled away, and no place was found for them. And I saw the dead, great and small, standing before the throne, and books were opened… And if anyone's name was not found written in the book of life, he was thrown into the lake of fire. Then I saw a new heaven and a new earth, for the first heaven and the first earth had passed away, and the sea was no more. And I saw the holy city, new Jerusalem, coming down out of heaven from God, prepared as a bride adorned for her husband…

Revelation 20-21

Anticipating God's final judgment

1. Where do you hope to be in your life and faith when final judgment comes for you?

2. Review Hebrews 10:19-31 and then ask yourself, are you ready to face final judgment or do fears remain? Comment.

Heaven: Our Ultimate Destiny

3. How would you describe the substance and source of your fears or your confidence?

4. When you see troubles coming, what is your usual reaction, anger or joy? Would you like to develop more resilience and, if so, how?

5. Does the idea of final judgment have any hopeful aspects to it for you? List some of them with brief notes.

Be sure to review Revelation 20-22 closely for clear descriptions of this time period in while you're preparing to answer the above question.

Lesson 9F
What will happen on earth?

Understanding 7: Our eternal home – Journey. Casting a vision of where we will be after we die and how we can live our lives between now and then.

The changes our world will go through between now and the Second Coming of Christ, after His arrival, and through final judgment to our eternal destination.

This Lesson has to do with eschatology. Coming toward the end of our discipleship studies as it does, we have the advantage of all the reading and studying of God's Word we've already done along with our own observations about human nature and how history seems to unfold in the world around us. Let's review the three historical perspectives on the end times that we've outlined in our **Prophetic Views of The Millennium** handout, with a fourth one added from the secular world:

1. **Premillennialism.** This is the oldest interpretation, dating from the 1st Century, and foresees the world going through an increasingly intense sequence of "*tribulations*" or "*birth pangs*" culminating in a final Great Tribulation that will herald Christ's Second Coming and the beginning of the Millennial Reign.

2. **Amillennialism.** An interpretation developed as the Roman Church ascended and gained worldly power several hundred years later that envisions the Catholic Church replacing Israel as the "Millennial" manifestation of God's Kingdom on earth.

3. **Postmillennialism.** A much more recent interpretation which sees an evangelical movement steadily advancing God's Kingdom through the spread of the Gospel message until all peoples and their spheres of influence have been won to Christ, at which time Jesus will return and begin His Millennial reign.

4. ***Progressivism.*** Along with the above interpretations, a competing secular humanist vision has developed and been promoted in political realms over the past two or more centuries. This view foresees human reason and ingenuity steadily "progressing" and

creating a strong, worldwide, and lasting societal utopia without needing a god. This futuristic vision is carried in radical "left-wing" critical theory ideologies like Marxism as well as toxic "right-wing" ideological movements like National Socialism (Nazism).

For now, consider the possibility that the course of human history over the past two millennia has essentially invalidated Options 2 and 3 as follows. No matter how potent they may be, neither the Roman Church nor evangelical activities have demonstrated the capacity or track record of successfully overcoming deception and sin worldwide while God's adversary, Satan, remains active. Option 1 also actually foretells the spread and then utter defeat of Option 4's godless ideologies as well.

Will there be widespread tribulations of various kinds in various places here on earth between now and the Lord's Return? Most certainly. Will they get closer and more intense as time goes on? If they behave at all like "*birth pangs*" they surely will. Premillennialism validates prophecies about a seven-year period of Great Tribulation on the earth culminating with Armageddon, Christ's Second Coming, the binding of Satan, and the start of the Millennial Kingdom. Compare this with the suffering humanity was called upon to endure before and through WWII and the Holocaust. Will we be anxious or more like women who are able to embrace their "*birth pangs*" by looking forward to the joyful outcome?

In the Christian community today, a further controversy exists within Option 1 – will faithful, believing Christians be asked to endure the Great Tribulation or will they be "raptured" or snatched out sometime before or during the final years, as 1 Thessalonians 4:17 might suggest? This doctrine is one of several unusual ones in an alternate view of biblical history called "Dispensationalism" that has gained a significant following since being proposed by John Nelson Darby in 1830 and popularized by Clarence Larkin in 1918. You can read more about Dispensationalism in our handout entitled **One Pattern of History**.

There are many ins and outs to the "rapture" controversy, but consider "Pascal's Wager" (see Page 23) as you study: How ready will you be for Christ's return if you aren't "raptured out" but instead encounter and go through some serious tribulations on your way? Wisdom might suggest preparing for the worst and then being joyfully surprised when God's comfort and strength are there to sustain you, as David promises in Psalm 31 and Jesus's words on the Mount of Olives indicate:

Oh, how abundant is your goodness which you have stored up for those who fear you and worked for those who take refuge in you in the sight of the children of mankind! In the cover of your presence you hide them from the plots of men; you store them in your shelter from the strife of tongues.　　Psalm 31:19-20

As he sat on the Mount of Olives, the disciples came to him privately, saying, "Tell us, when will these things be, and what will be the sign of your coming and of the end of the age?" And Jesus answered them, "See that no one leads you astray. For many will come in my name, saying, 'I am the Christ,' and they will lead many astray. And you will hear of wars and rumors of wars. See that you are not alarmed, for this must take place, but the end is not yet. For nation will rise against nation, and kingdom against kingdom, and there will be famines and earthquakes in various places. All these are but the beginning of the birth pains. Then they will deliver you up to tribulation and put you to death, and you will be hated by all nations for my name's sake. And then many will fall away and betray one another and hate one another. And many false prophets will arise and lead many astray. And because lawlessness will be increased, the love of many will grow cold. But the one who endures to the end will be saved. And this gospel of the kingdom will be proclaimed throughout the whole world as a testimony to all nations, and then the end will come.　　Matthew 24:3-14

Letting the Word guide our hopes and imaginations

1. James 1:2-4 reasons with us to *"Count it all joy, my brothers, when you meet trials of various kinds."* Can you approach tribulation this way?

2. As you read God's Word about the end of the age, what questions do you have? Can you find any verses that shed light on them?

Heaven: Our Ultimate Destiny

3. How much of the earth and its population does the Word say will be directly afflicted by the Great Tribulation? Site some references.

4. When Jesus asked the question *"When the Son of Man comes, will he find faith on earth?"* in Luke 18:8 what answer was He expecting?

5. What kinds of things can you imagine happening as the world is restored during the anointed times of the Millennial Kingdom?

Consider rereading our Kingdom handout **Prophetic Views of The Millennium** in light of Corrie ten Boom's testimony (see Page 60). Then review **Discourse on the End Times** from Lesson 7 and **One Pattern of History** online at https://www.celebratesalvation.org/more/#2.

Understanding 7: Journey   Lesson 9F

Lesson 10F
Can we hasten our Lord's return?

Understanding 7: Our eternal home – Journey. Casting a vision of where we will be after we die and how we can live our lives between now and then.

Many translations of 2 Peter 3 (esp. verse 12) might suggest that our actions may have an effect on when the Lord will return. What does Peter mean?

Let's look closely at what Peter wrote in the third chapter of his second Epistle to the Christians in Asia Minor in the ESV translation:

This is now the second letter that I am writing to you, beloved. In both of them I am stirring up your sincere mind by way of reminder, that you should remember the predictions of the holy prophets and the commandment of the Lord and Savior through your apostles, knowing this first of all, that **scoffers will come in the last days** *with scoffing, following their own sinful desires. They will say, "Where is the promise of his coming? For ever since the fathers fell asleep, all things are continuing as they were from the beginning of creation." For they deliberately overlook this fact, that the heavens existed long ago, and the earth was formed out of water and through water by the word of God, and that by means of these the world that then existed was deluged with water and perished. But by the same word the heavens and earth that now exist are stored up for fire, being kept until the day of judgment and destruction of the ungodly.*

But do not overlook this one fact, beloved, that with the Lord one day is as a thousand years, and a thousand years as one day. **The Lord is not slow** *to fulfill his promise as some count slowness,* **but is patient toward you**, *not wishing that any should perish, but that all should reach repentance. But* **the day of the Lord will come like a thief**, *and then the heavens will pass away with a roar, and the heavenly bodies will be burned up and dissolved, and the earth and the works that are done on it will be exposed.*

Since all these things are thus to be dissolved, what sort of people ought you to be in lives of holiness and godliness, waiting for and **hastening the coming of the day of God**,* because of which the heavens will be set on fire and dissolved, and the heavenly bodies will melt as they burn! But according to his*

Heaven: Our Ultimate Destiny

promise we are waiting for new heavens and a new earth in which righteousness dwells.

Therefore, beloved, since **you are waiting** *for these, be diligent to be found by him without spot or blemish, and at peace. And count the patience of our Lord as salvation, just as our beloved brother Paul also wrote to you according to the wisdom given him, as he does in all his letters when he speaks in them of these matters. There are some things in them that are* **hard to understand**, *which the ignorant and unstable twist to their own destruction, as they do the other Scriptures. You therefore, beloved, knowing this beforehand, take care that you are not carried away with* **the error of lawless people** *and lose your own stability. But grow in the grace and knowledge of our Lord and Savior Jesus Christ. To him be the glory both now and to the day of eternity. Amen.*

* The word Peter used in verse 12 for "*hastening*" is σπεύδοντας or *speudontas* in the underlying Greek, which Strong's Concordance tells us comes from a root that often means "to hasten" or "urge on." The Strong's notes that follow, however, identify that an equally valid and appropriate translation for this passage could be "to desire earnestly." Although these two translations might seem quite different, they can be reconciled faithfully by a process that Christopher Watkin, author of the insightful book *Biblical Critical Theory*, calls "diagonalizing" when we take into account how God responds to our earnest prayers.

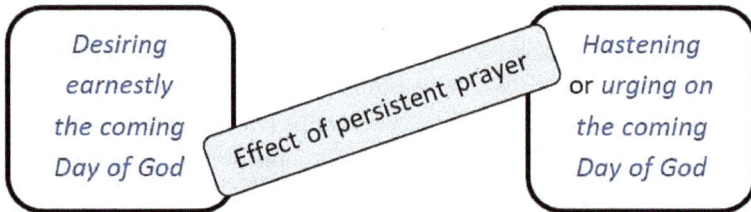

Desiring earnestly the coming Day of God — Effect of persistent prayer — Hastening or urging on the coming Day of God

Shortly after sharing the Lord's Prayer with His disciples in Luke 11, Jesus told the Parable of the Friend at Night, which carries a message about the value of believers praying without giving up that is similar to the Parable of the Importunate Widow in Luke 18. He goes on to say

And I tell you, ask, and it will be given to you; seek, and you will find; knock, and it will be opened to you. For everyone who asks receives, and the one who seeks finds, and to the one who knocks it will be opened.   Luke 11:9-10

Remarkably, all three of the verbs used in this exhortation – *ask*, *seek*, and *knock* – are in the Greek "imperative present tense" which renders the persistent nature of the command, as in "*ask and keep on asking*" for that which is in keeping with God's will, as John indicates:

I write these things to you who believe in the name of the Son of God, that you may know that you have eternal life. And this is the confidence that we have toward him, that if we ask anything according to his will he hears us. And if we know that he hears us in whatever we ask, we know that we have the requests that we have asked of him.   1 John 5:13-15

The combination of these understandings indicates that if we know God's will through His Word and the inner witness of His Holy Spirit and pray earnestly for His will to be done here *on earth as it is in heaven*, then He will expedite our intercessions.

And let us consider how to stir up one another to love and good works, not neglecting to meet together, as is the habit of some, but encouraging one another, and all the more as you see the Day drawing near.   Hebrews 10:24–25

Can we both *earnestly desire* and *hasten* the Lord's coming simultaneously through prayer? Yes! ***Maranatha! Come, Lord Jesus!***

Looking forward to the Lord's return

1. Do you believe that God hears and answers our prayers? How could this "*hasten*" His return?

2. Do you have a clear vision of the "*coming day of God*"? If so, what would hold you back from "desiring earnestly" to see it come?

Heaven: Our Ultimate Destiny

50

3. Do you have any prayer requests for your family or friends that you've been hoping He will answer before He returns in glory?

4. What parts of your own life are you hoping and praying for the Lord to change before or when He returns?

5. What aspects of the world today are you hoping and praying for the Lord to change before or when He returns?

As you contemplate how you can get into an attitude of ongoing prayer, you might enjoy handout on **How to Pray without Ceasing**, available online at https://www.celebratesalvation.org/more/#2.

Lesson 11F
What about life between now and then?

Understanding 7: Our eternal home – Journey. Casting a vision of where we will be after we die and how we can live our lives between now and then.

Living in eternal life now while looking forward to both the promise of the Millennial Kingdom and the new heavens and new earth to follow.

The years of our life are seventy, or even by reason of strength eighty; so teach us to number our days that we may get a heart of wisdom.   Psalm 90:10, 12

The way we respond to the challenge of how to spend the rest of our lives, depends to some degree on how much time we think we have left. Certainly the Lord's Second Coming is a long way off, right? Younger people tend to think that time is elastic and that they have lots of time left to figure things out. Surprisingly, older people aren't much different. Perhaps those of us who are reaching or beyond the usual "retirement age" should read and ponder Atul Gawande's bestselling book *Being Mortal: Medicine and What Matters in the End*. How old are you? How close to the Lord's Second Coming and/or your own death are you? The fact of the matter is that, although delay is likely, either one could happen anytime, suddenly and without warning:

Behold! I tell you a mystery. We shall not all sleep, but we shall all be changed, in a moment, in the twinkling of an eye, at the last trumpet. For the trumpet will sound, and the dead will be raised imperishable, and we shall be changed.

1 Corinthians 15:51-52

New Testament Greek distinguishes two kinds of time, *chronos* (used 54 times) and *kairos* (used 86 times). Essentially *chronos* refers to clock or calendar time in this world, while *kairos* speaks of "the right, critical, or opportune moments" of time. God created and inhabits all of time, but calls us to be spiritually with Him moment by moment so that we are always in the right place at the right time to discern and do His will. So let's tune in to His *kairos* time in our lives and stay there as we seek to

Heaven: Our Ultimate Destiny

discern what we need to get straight between now and His return. The most important areas are those noted in His "greatest commandments" – our *agape* love relationships with God, ourselves, and others.

Do you genuinely love God "*with all your heart and with all your soul and with all your mind*"? In other words, have you been "*born again*" by turning from your disorderly ways and committing your life entirely to Him and His ways? Have you received His forgiveness, made a public confession of faith, been baptized, and asked to receive the fullness of His Holy Spirit? Are your relationships with yourself, your family and friends, and those around you in good order? Have you asked Him to search your heart to "*see if there be any grievous way*" in you, and cleanse or sanctify you "*in the way everlasting*"? What "unfinished buisiness" is left? As Paul notes, "*Behold, now is the favorable time [kairos]; behold, now is the day of salvation.*" As you ponder, take some time to reread and meditate on Peter's full instructions to us in his first Epistle.

Life in this world is both rewarding and challenging. It has its ups and downs. Perhaps the best way to gauge how a person is doing overall is to see how they handle the stressful trials and tribulations of life. Are you growing in faith and its qualities, as Peter described in the first chapter of his second Epistle, and bearing the fruit of the Spirit outlined by Paul in his letter to the Galatian church?

The fruit of the Spirit is love, joy, peace, patience, kindness, goodness, faithfulness, gentleness, self-control; against such things there is no law. Galatians 5:22-23

As "the end" approaches we will need to draw more and more on two commodities that only God can supply, His wisdom and His strength.

If any of you lacks wisdom, let him ask God, who gives generously to all without reproach, and it will be given him… for the joy of the LORD is your strength.

James 1:5 *and* Nehemiah 8:10

Count it all joy, my brothers, when you meet trials of various kinds, for you know that the testing of your faith produces steadfastness. And let steadfastness have its full effect, that you may be perfect and complete, lacking in nothing.

James 1:2-4

Not only that, but we rejoice in our sufferings, knowing that suffering produces endurance, and endurance produces character, and character produces hope, and hope does not put us to shame, because God's love has been poured into our hearts through the Holy Spirit who has been given to us. Romans 5:3-5

Since therefore Christ suffered in the flesh, arm yourselves with the same way of thinking, for whoever has suffered in the flesh has ceased from sin, so as to live for the rest of the time in the flesh no longer for human passions but for the will of God.

1 Peter 4:1-2

I can do all things through him who strengthens me, **but** *apart from [him] you can do nothing.*

Philippians 4:13 **and** John 15:5

In summary, according to Pastor Chuck Swindoll all of what we're looking at is a manifestion of our underlying attitude toward God, ourselves, others, and life itself. Years ago he wrote a brief summary, available as part of our **Attitude Checklists** worksheet and handout. As you look forward, take time to read our handout and do some introspection in preparation for making a full personal inventory of your strengths and remaining weaknesses. Consider that you're about to go on a strenuous journey between now and your full inheritance of God's promises, and then start developing a plan for getting into shape!

Organizing my priorities for the future

1. Is your sense of eternal salvation secure? List some of your life experiences and commitments that support your confidence.

2. What areas of your life are you still having trouble with? List some of your plans for dealing with these.

Heaven: Our Ultimate Destiny

54

3. Do you have any concerns for the future? Name some of them, along with the outcomes you are praying for.

4. Do either you or others think your attitude needs to be adjusted? What are some of the behaviors and issues behind these concerns?

5. List some of your most solid hopes and promises about eternal life, both immediately after death and on into eternity.

Be sure to study our handout **Attitude Checklists**, available online at https://www.celebratesalvation.org/more/#2, and make notes on its worksheets for reference as you respond to our questions above.

Lesson 12F
How should we then live?

Understanding 7: Our eternal home – Journey. Casting a vision of where we will be after we die and how we can live our lives between now and then.

Examining our gifts and calling closely for signs about how the Lord would want us to prepare for our lives leading into and beyond His Second Coming.

Where there is no prophetic vision the people cast off restraint, but blessed is he who keeps the law.
Proverbs 29:18

Pursue love, and earnestly desire the spiritual gifts, especially that you may prophesy... for the one who prophesies speaks to people for their upbuilding and encouragement and consolation.
1 Corinthians 14:1,3

What are spiritual gifts, especially the gift of prophecy?

Prophecy is one spiritual gift among many other gifts given by God to his *Ekklesia*, His called out people, His Bride. The spiritual gifts are special abilities given to us through the power of the Holy Spirit, which are meant to bless the Body of Christ, and the world as a whole. Paul listed eight of them in his first letter to the Corinthians as follows: wisdom, words of knowledge, faith, gifts of healings, working of miracles, prophecy, discerning of spirits, speaking in tongues, and interpretation of tongues. Of these, the gift of speaking in tongues is noted by Paul to be the most basic, followed by prophecy.

It may surprise you in this day when common sense has become far from common, that the gifts of tongues and prophecy are readily available, while other gifts like healings and miracles are less ordinary. Still others may erroneously appear to be more esoteric and possibly even irrelevant in today's world.

So, what exactly is the gift of prophecy? In simple terms, prophecy is the ability to **hear** the voice of God and, by extension, to follow in its guidance. In the verb form, to prophesy (spelled with an "s" instead of a "c") means to **speak** with the words and voice of God to edify others with messages of love, conviction, encouragement, guidance, and wisdom. In the words of a once popular song, "What the world needs now is love, sweet love: it's the only thing that there's just too little of." How do we receive and share God's love? By hearing His voice and following through with action. This is prophecy, without which people go astray, each seeking their own lawless way. Does that sound familiar?

As believers in the life, death, resurrection, and witness of Jesus, we've all been offered gifts to use in advancing His Kingdom, both now and in the Millennial Age to come.

For the grace of God has appeared, bringing salvation for all people, training us to renounce ungodliness and worldly passions, and to live self-controlled, upright, and godly lives in the present age, waiting for our blessed hope, the appearing of the glory of our great God and Savior Jesus Christ, who gave himself for us to redeem us from all lawlessness and to purify for himself a people for his own possession who are zealous for good works.   Titus 2:11-14

The gifts we've been given are for doing things, which raises questions about what each one of us is being called to do. In other words, what are our callings? We can clearly identify those who are called to serve as leaders in the gathered church. Ephesians 4:11-12 identifies these as *apostles, prophets, evangelists, pastors* and *teachers*, whose task is *to equip his people for works of service, so that the body of Christ may be built up.* As you can see, most of us are listed among those called upon to help others in *works of service* or "administration" (which means "ministering to" others). What are you good and fruitful at doing? Where do you find joy? What do other people call upon or rely on you to help them with?

Find out who you are as a "human being" and what you're best at as a "human doing" and you're getting pretty close to your calling. Then seek the Lord to grow in any gifts He has for you that would help you carry out your calling. Which one is the most helpful of all? Being able to hear His voice and share what He's told you with others. That's prophecy, and upon the exercise of it the Kingdom of God will come and be built *on earth as it is in Heaven.*

Make a wish list; check it over not just twice but daily; open yourself wide to receive; and take hold of what God has for you. Keep notes; practice and refine what you hear; learn to flow in the Holy Spirit as part of God's solution to your own and this world's problems, and He will be with you in all you do. Actually, that's all He's asking for.

The Holy Spirit isn't in a separate faraway place but is present and active in and all around us, as Luke reports in Acts 17:28: *In Him we live and move and have our being.* The Spirit is ever-present sustaining the universe in order, sharing God the Father's "common" grace of wisdom and love, convicting us of our sin and His righteousness, and leading us as we grow in faith and share His love with those in our midst.

> *He ordered them not to depart from Jerusalem, but to wait for the promise of the Father, which, he said, "you heard from me; for John baptized with water, but you will be baptized with the Holy Spirit not many days from now."*
>
> Acts 1:4-5

Pray earnestly for an outpouring of His Holy Spirit within and around you, your family, your neighborhood, community, nation, and world. Study His Word regularly, opening your ears to receive His guidance, letting the joy of the Lord fill your sails with His attitude and strength, and LIVING in eternity with Him right here and now and on into the Millennial Kingdom and beyond! *The Spirit and the Bride say, "Come." And let the one who hears say, "Come." He who testifies to these things says, "Surely I am coming soon."* **Amen. Come, Lord Jesus!** Revelation 22:17, 20

Letting God take charge of our lives and future

1. Make a preliminary list with ideas about who you are and what kind of things you feel called to do:

2. Similarly list the gifts you currently feel you've received and are growing in as well as others you might be interested in.

Heaven: Our Ultimate Destiny

3. How do you see your life and faith developing in the remaining time you are likely to have here on earth?

4. What thoughts do you have about what life might be like for you in the Millennial Kingdom?

5. Make a prayerful list below of the areas in your life that you'll be seeking God's help with after you complete this study.

Rejoice always, pray without ceasing, give thanks in all circumstances; for this is the will of God in Christ Jesus for you. Do not quench the Spirit. Do not despise prophecies, but test everything; hold fast what is good. Abstain from every form of evil. Now may the God of peace himself sanctify you completely, and may your whole spirit and soul and body be kept blameless at the coming of our Lord Jesus Christ. He who calls you is faithful; he will surely do it. 1 Thessalonians 5:16-24

Commendation

Therefore let us leave the elementary doctrine of Christ and go on to maturity, not laying again a foundation of repentance from dead works and of faith toward God, and of instruction about washings, the laying on of hands, the resurrection of the dead, and eternal judgment. And this we will do if God permits.

Hebrews 6:1-3

Congratulations! We've just opened up what it is to look forward to death, resurrection, and Heaven in this, the final study in our *Joy of Christian Discipleship Series* (see Page 61). Throughout our *Series* we've been covering the *elementary doctrine* or foundations of our faith outlined above. The first four topics were dealt with in the three study guides of **Course 1** entitled *Saved, Sanctified,* and *Sent.* And now, after *going on to maturity* in **Course 2** with study guides *Awakening* and *Kingdom,* we've taken up the last two topics in the *Series* in this study on *Heaven.*

During the twenty centuries between when John completed the Bible with the Book of Revelation and now, mankind has undergone some dramatic changes, especially during the last two and a half. Much of what we've just studied together in *Heaven* was considered by early believers to be common, foundational knowledge, while many of the insights in *Awakening* and *Kingdom* were less obvious. Sadly, we've let go of many of the basics along the way. How difficult is this material? Compared with standard ways of categorizing learning, are our studies at the 8th grade, 12th grade, college, or graduate school level? Frankly, all of them are pretty basic, leaving us plenty of room to learn and grow!

Now what? Our entire lives lie ahead of us in a world that's hungry for God's Word. Let's keep what we've learned in mind and draw close to Him as we investigate what's involved in living for Christ and His Kingdom while we join Him in carrying out His Great Commission!

And Jesus came and said to them, "All authority in heaven and on earth has been given to me. Go therefore and make disciples of all nations, baptizing them in the name of the Father and of the Son and of the Holy Spirit, teaching them to observe all that I have commanded you. And behold, I am with you always, to the end of the age."

Matthew 28:18-20

He who testifies to these things says, "Surely I am coming soon." Amen. Come, Lord Jesus!

Revelation 22:20

Heaven: Our Ultimate Destiny

Suggestions for Further Study

The Holy Bible
English Standard Version® ESV Study Bible™.

Dante Alighieri
The Divine Comedy: The Inferno, The Purgatorio, The Paradiso.

Corrie ten Boom – *In My Father's House: The Years Before "The Hiding Place."* Living faithfully during ongoing tribulation.

Atul Gawande – *Being Mortal: Medicine and What Matters in the End.* Strong on aging, but weak on preparing for afterlife.

Todd Hampson – *The Non-Prophet's Guide to the End Times.* Very helpful overall but with some Dispensational speculations.

Michael Heiser – *The Unseen Realm: Recovering the Supernatural Worldview of the Bible.*

Timothy Keller, R. Albert Mohler, J. I. Packer, et al. *Is Hell for Real or Does Everyone Go to Heaven?*

C. S. Lewis – *The Great Divorce, a Dream.* An allegorical fantasy.

Derek Prince – *War in Heaven.* *The Foundation Series, a set of 7 booklets.*

Francis Schaeffer – *How Should We Then Live: The Rise and Decline of Western Thought and Culture.*

Randall B. Smith – *From Here to Eternity: Reflections on Death, Immortality, and the Resurrection of the Body.*

Christopher Watkin
Biblical Critical Theory: How the Bible's Unfolding Story Makes Sense of Modern Life and Culture.

Michael E. Wittmer, Editor
Four Views on Heaven.

Notes and References

Additional Celebrate Salvation® Resources

Books in the Joy of Christian Discipleship Series

The Joy of Christian Discipleship Course 1

> Established in 3 Stages and 7 Steps, a 36-week group study

1. **A - Saved!** *Rescued by Grace*
2. **B - Sanctified:** *Coming Clean with God*
3. **C - Sent:** *Becoming a Living Letter*

   Plus - Handouts and Worksheets *or* **Complete Course 1**

An 8-week Devotional Guide to 3 Stages and 7 Steps

4. **Essentials of the Christian Faith:**
   7 Steps to Abundant Life, an 8-week daily devotional guide

The Joy of Christian Discipleship Course 2

> Equipped in 3 Realms with 7 Understandings, a 36-week group
> study for Christians who are established in their faith

5. **D - Awakening:** *The Triumph of Truth*
6. **E - Kingdom:** *God's Reign in our Midst*
7. **F - Heaven:** *Our Ultimate Destiny* (this book)

   Heaven Handouts *

   > Translation of *Ouranos and* Three Realms of the Heavens (2F)
   > Heaven in a Biblical Perspective *and* Heavenly Imaginations (3F)
   > End Times Scripture References (3F)
   > Mormon Kingdoms *and* Alternative Views of the Afterlife (4F)
   > Biblical Timetable/Bookends *and* Eternity, Infinity, and God (5F)
   > Purgatory and Paradise (6F) *and* End Times Discourse (7F)
   > Prophetic Views of the Millennium (9E Kingdom handout)
   > One Pattern of History (9F)
   > Prayer Without Ceasing (10F) *and* Attitude Checklists (11F)

   Plus – Handouts and Worksheets or **Complete Course 2**

*Links to all Handouts in printable PDF form as well as Additional
Resources can be found online at www.celebratesalvation.org/more/#2.

Another Kingdom Press Book by Dr. Morehouse

The Biblical Festivals, *including A Passover Seder*

Notes